Reading Essentials
in Science

CHEMISTRY CLUES

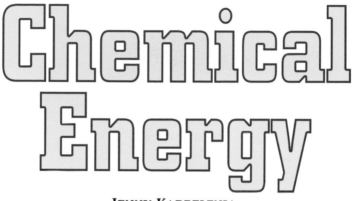

Chemical Energy

JENNY KARPELENIA

PERFECTION LEARNING®

Editorial Director: Susan C. Thies
Editor: Mary L. Bush
Design Director: Randy Messer
Book Design: Emily J. Greazel
Cover Design: Michael A. Aspengren

A special thanks to the following for his scientific review of the book: Kristin
Mandsager, Instructor of Physics and Astronomy, North Iowa Area Community College

Image credits:
©Associated Press: p. 24; ©Bettmann/CORBIS: pp. 9, 17; ©Hulton-Deutsch Collection/CORBIS:
p. 13 (bottom); ©David Woods/CORBIS: p. 14; ©Jeffrey L. Rotman/CORBIS: p. 26; ©Constantinos
Petrinos/naturepl.com: p. 25; ©Doug Wechsler/naturepl.com: p. 27

©Royalty-Free/CORBIS: pp. 11, 19; Perfection Learning: pp. 6 (top), 7, 10, 12, 15, 16, 18, 20,
21 (illustration), 22; Photos.com: cover, pp. 1, 3, 4, 5, 6 (bottom), 13 (top), 20–21 (background), 29

For information, contact
Perfection Learning® Corporation
1000 North Second Avenue, P.O. Box 500
Logan, Iowa 51546-0500.
Phone: 1-800-831-4190
Fax: 1-800-543-2745
perfectionlearning.com

1 2 3 4 5 6 PP 10 09 08 07 06 05

Paperback ISBN 0-7891-6616-x
Reinforced Library Binding ISBN 0-7569-4640-9

Contents

CHAPTER 1

Lots of Energy

Your alarm clock goes off in the morning, and you reluctantly roll out of bed and hit the shower. Why does school have to start so early? Why couldn't it wait until noon? By then you'd have enough **energy** to tackle the classes, projects, and homework. Right now, you barely have enough energy to get dressed.

What is this energy that comes and goes? How can you get it when you need it?

Energy is the ability to do work or to get things done. It is the ability to accomplish a task or make something happen. Everything has or uses energy. People and plants use energy to grow and change. Machines use energy to get a job done. Without energy, nothing in the world would work.

Energy has several forms. Light, heat, sound, motion, electrical, atomic/nuclear, and chemical are all types of energy. All kinds of energy can change from one form to another. Motion energy can change to sound energy. **Chemical energy** can change to light and heat energy. When you eat lunch, your body changes the chemical energy in the food into motion energy to move and heat energy to keep you warm. These energy changes happen all around you every day.

POTENTIAL OR KINETIC?

At any given moment, energy can be stored or used. Stored energy is called *potential energy*. An object at rest has potential energy. The energy a body has when it's moving is called *kinetic energy*. All moving objects have kinetic energy.

Has anyone ever told you that you have the potential to do something? Perhaps your teacher says you have the potential to be a good student or your coach says you have the potential to become a professional ball player. Having potential means that you have the ability to do something, but you aren't doing it at the moment. It's the same with potential energy. For example, an unlit match has the potential to burn, but until it's lit, it's just storing chemical energy in the head of the match. A **battery** sitting on a shelf has the potential to power a video game. However, until it's placed in the game and the game is turned on, it's just potential energy.

Energy in action is kinetic energy. When a match is lit, gases are produced and move very quickly. They have kinetic energy. These moving gases give off light. When the video game is played, the battery's potential energy becomes electrical energy.

5

CHEMICAL ENERGY

Chemical energy is the energy held within **chemicals**. Chemicals are the basic substances that make up all things. Some chemicals are single **elements** found in nature, such as hydrogen and oxygen. Other chemicals are a combination of elements. For example, the elements sodium and chlorine combine to form the chemical sodium chloride.

The **atoms** and **molecules** that make up chemicals are held together by **chemical bonds**.

SODIUM CHLORIDE MOLECULES

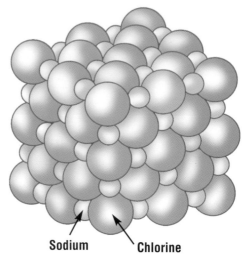

Sodium   Chlorine

Chemical energy is stored in these bonds. When the bonds are broken and new ones are formed, chemical energy changes. The process of breaking and forming chemical bonds to create new substances is called a **chemical reaction**. Chemical energy may increase or decrease as a result of these reactions. If the chemical energy decreases, that means it has changed to a different form of energy. This transformation of chemical energy occurs in humans, plants, fuels, batteries, and machines. It helps us get things done!

CHAPTER 2

Burning Up

I magine sitting around a campfire on a chilly autumn
night. Your feet warm up as you watch the yellow and
orange flames dancing in the night. The fire is a perfect
example of chemical energy changing into heat and light
energy. Sometimes you even hear sound energy popping
and crackling from the fire.

A BURNING TRIANGLE

Combustion, or burning, is a common use of
chemical energy. Burning changes the chemical energy
present in a material such as gas or wood to light and
heat energy. This energy can then provide light and heat
for people and places.

In order for combustion to occur and a fire to
exist, three items must be present and interact.
These items are fuel, oxygen, and heat.
Together, these three elements form a fire
triangle. If one of these three materials is
missing, a fire cannot start. If one of
them is removed from a burning fire,
the fire will go out.

A fuel is any substance that has
the potential to burn. Some examples of common fuels
are wood, gasoline, coal, natural gas, and oil. A fuel stores
its chemical energy until it's exposed to enough heat and
oxygen to ignite, or start on fire. Once the reaction starts,
the heat produced becomes the heat source needed to
keep the reaction going.

7

Oxygen is a gas that makes up about one-fifth of the air you breathe. Just like you need oxygen to live, fuels need oxygen to burn. Oxygen in the air combines with **flammable vapors** given off by fuels. When a spark or flame is added, combustion occurs.

A heat source is needed to ignite a fire. A match, candle, lighter, or other flaming or sparking object will do the job.

Heat is also needed to create flammable vapors from solids. A piece of wood, for example, must be heated in order to give off the vapors that mix with oxygen and can then be ignited by additional heat. Some liquids must also be heated to create vapors, but others give off vapors even when they're cool. Flammable gases are already in vapor form. They just need a flame or spark to ignite them.

A FIERY EXAMPLE

Let's use the campfire example to follow the process of combustion. Wood is made of a substance called *cellulose*, which is made of carbon, hydrogen, and oxygen. Cellulose vaporizes when heated. Part of the heated fuel (firewood) becomes a gas. This gas mixes with the oxygen in the air. As the wood continues to heat up, it eventually reaches its ignition point. This is the temperature at which a fuel is hot enough for its chemical bonds to break. At this point, the fuel will ignite and a fire will break out.

The fire gives off light and heat energy. The heat energy keeps the fire burning. Until one of the items from the fire triangle is removed, the fire will continue to burn.

How do you put out your campfire? If you have time, you can let the fire go until all of the wood has burned. This removes the fuel source from the triangle. But if you need to go to bed or leave camp before this happens, you have other options. Cooling the fire with water will eliminate the heat element in the triangle, causing the fire to go out. Covering the fire with dirt, sand, or foam from a fire extinguisher will keep oxygen from reaching the fire. Without oxygen, the fire triangle is broken.

CONVENIENT COMBUSTION

Since early times, people have tried to invent machines that safely burn a fuel to produce heat or motion energy. Combustion machines convert chemical energy to heat energy. Often this heat energy is then changed to kinetic, or motion, energy.

Combustion inventions have changed since first being devised more than 2000 years ago. Around 100 B.C., a Greek man named Hero invented an aeolipile (ee OH lee peyel). This small device used steam to turn a globe over a pot of boiling water. During his time, Hero's invention was never used as anything more than an entertaining toy. However, it later became a model for more advanced steam engines.

The first true steam engine was invented in 1698 by an Englishman named Thomas Savery. It was an external combustion engine. This type of engine burns fuel outside the engine. Steam engines were used to run machines, boats, and trains throughout the 1700s.

Scientist of Significance

James Watt did not invent the steam engine. He did, however, make significant improvements to the engine, making it much more useful. Watt was a Scottish inventor and engineer who figured out how to make steam engines run more efficiently. As a result, the use of steam engines boomed, which led to the **Industrial Revolution**.

Watt invented several parts that revolutionized the use of steam engines. He made the machines more effective, powerful, and reliable. Many of his principles are still used today in modern inventions.

In honor of his work, the electrical unit of power called the *watt* was named after this important scientist.

The internal combustion engine was invented in the 1800s. This type of engine burns fuel inside the engine. Gasoline is a common fuel used in these engines, but they can also be powered by diesel, propane, methane, or hydrogen.

The early internal combustion engines invented by Francois Issac de Rivas of Switzerland and Samuel Morey of the United States were impractical. It wasn't until 1858 that Belgian engineer Jean Lenoir invented a useful version using coal gas. About ten years later, several scientists began designing and building internal combustion engines to be used in cars.

In a typical car engine, gasoline and air are sprayed into the engine's cylinders. A piston inside each cylinder pushes on the gasoline/air mixture. A spark given off by a spark plug ignites the fuel. The hot gases from the combustion reaction then push the piston back down. The waste gases are given off as exhaust, and the cycle starts all over again. The up-and-down motion of the pistons is changed into a circular (rotary) motion by the crankshaft. The crankshaft then rotates the wheels of the car.

FOUR-CYCLE ENGINE

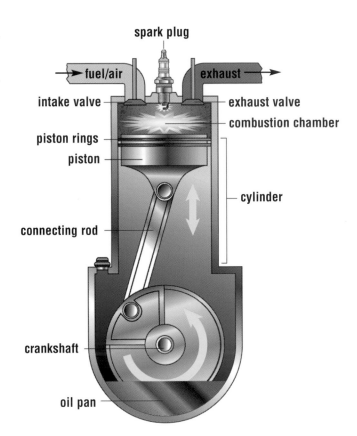

spark plug

fuel/air — exhaust —

intake valve — exhaust valve

— combustion chamber

piston rings —

piston —

— cylinder

connecting rod —

crankshaft —

oil pan —

Internal combustion engines are also used for chain saws, lawn mowers, motorcycles, trucks, trains, jets, and rockets. All of these machines burn their fuel inside the engine.

Combustion Comfort

Oil and gas furnaces are other combustion inventions that keep your home a comfortable temperature in cold weather. Burning gas or oil heats up air flowing through the furnace. The warm air then moves through ducts to other areas of the house. Even houses that use electric heaters may rely on chemical energy used by the energy company to power their electric generators. So thank chemical energy the next time your furnace is keeping you warm on a chilly night!

CHAPTER 3

Kaboom!

Picture a beautiful display of fireworks on the Fourth of July. Can you see the bright colors shooting through the sky and hear the loud popping and banging sounds as the fireworks burst in the air? These spectacular displays of light are the result of chemical energy.

EXPLOSIVE INFORMATION

An **explosion** is a sudden release of a large amount of energy. Combustion often leads to explosions. When burning takes place inside a closed chamber, the heat causes the fuel to expand. The atoms in the fuel spread apart, taking up more room. The gas atoms push against the chamber walls, building pressure in the closed chamber. When the gas is released, it explodes out of the chamber with great force.

This is what happens with fireworks. Hot gases burning within the fireworks build up pressure. When the fireworks finally explode, the chemical energy inside is changed to light, heat, motion, and sound energy. All of this energy is released quickly, producing the brilliant display of light, color, and sound.

INSIDE A FIREWORK

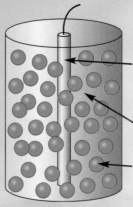

Bursting charge packed with black powder

Black powder (gunpowder)

Stars made of explosive material that bursts into colorful light

The size of chemical explosions varies greatly. An internal combustion engine, such as in a car engine, creates mini-explosions to move the car. Firearms produce small explosions that propel the bullets toward a target. Rocket boosters use much larger explosions to launch rockets into space.

EXPLOSIVE MATERIALS

Explosives are materials that are designed to produce explosions to accomplish a task. Gunpowder, also known as black powder, was invented around 1000 A.D. It was used by the Chinese for fireworks and for scaring away enemies. In the mid-1800s, nitroglycerine and nitrocellulose were first used as explosives. Trinitrotoluene (TNT) was an explosive used in World War I (1914–1918) to attack enemies. Since the early 1900s, many other explosive substances have been found.

Mine fields in France during World War I

Explosives are grouped as either low or high. Low explosives burn at a slower speed and create more of a pushing (propellant) force. In these explosives, the hot gases produced from the chemical reaction have an escape route. Low explosives are useful for pushing bullets out of guns, propelling rockets into space, or separating large chunks of rock in quarries and mines.

High explosives burn much faster and create more of a blasting (detonating) force. There is no escape route for the gases produced by the chemical reaction, so when the pressure gets too great, the gases explode forcefully in all directions. Dynamite is an example of a high explosive. Demolition teams on road-building crews and in rock quarries use high explosives to shatter rock into smaller pieces.

Technology Link

One safety device that uses explosives is a car air bag. A low explosive called *sodium azide* is placed inside the air bag. This chemical is a combination of sodium and nitrogen (NaN_3). When the car crashes, a chemical reaction is set in motion. The sodium separates from the nitrogen. The nitrogen molecules pair off to form nitrogen gas, which fills the air bag quickly. This explosive invention can be a lifesaver for adults.

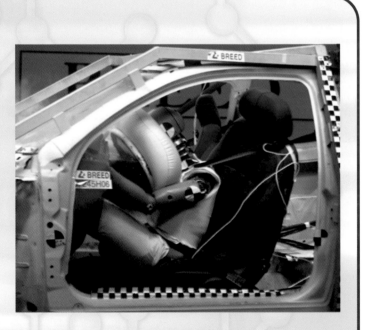

CHAPTER 4

Get Charged Up

How many times have you opened a present and found it wouldn't work without batteries? That new video game or portable CD player doesn't do you much good without the batteries required. So you throw in a few batteries and you're set. But did you ever stop to think about how those batteries worked?

A battery is a device that stores chemical energy. When a chemical reaction occurs within the battery, the chemical energy changes to electrical energy. This electrical energy powers the gadget that holds the battery.

The chemical reaction inside a battery is triggered by the flow of tiny negative particles called *electrons*. These particles can only move when a circuit, or path, is complete. Batteries have two ends, or terminals. One terminal is positive (+) and one is negative (–). When a wire connects the two terminals, the circuit is closed, or complete. Electrons in the wire can then flow away from the negative terminal toward the positive terminal. The wire is also attached to the device that the battery is powering. The flow of electrons through the wire transfers electrical power from the battery to operate the object.

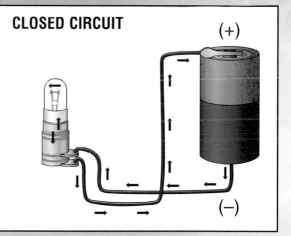

CLOSED CIRCUIT
(+)
(–)

Because the chemical reaction inside a battery only starts once the circuit is complete, batteries can be stored for a long time and still work. The chemical energy isn't used until the battery is placed in a device and the flow of electrons begins.

Once the chemicals inside a battery are used up, the battery stops moving the electrons. Some batteries can be recharged. An electrical recharging device can reverse the normal chemical reaction and produce the necessary chemicals.

Much of your life is dependent on the chemical energy found in batteries. The car that takes you where you want to go, the cell phone you use to talk to your friends, the handheld game you play when you're supposed to be studying—all of these rely on batteries to power them. A lot of work is done by those tiny round or square power cells!

Tracing the Path of Science

Batteries have existed for thousands of years. A primitive battery from 200 B.C. was found in Iraq. The battery consisted of a large clay jar containing an iron rod surrounded by a copper tube. The jar had traces of vinegar inside it. This combination of materials is now known to form a battery.

It wasn't until 1800, though, that a modern battery was invented. Alessandro Volta was an Italian scientist who made the first battery out of layers of zinc, copper, and paper soaked with salt water. The electrical unit of voltage called the *volt* was named after Volta.

Alessandro Volta

After Volta's invention, scientists continued to experiment with different materials to create batteries. The lead-acid battery was invented in 1859 by French scientist Gaston Plante. This type of battery is still used in cars today.

In the 1860s, French scientist George Leclanche invented the "dry cell" battery. This battery didn't require a layer of liquid like the first batteries had. Many types of dry cell batteries were invented in the years that followed. These include zinc-carbon, alkaline, and lithium-ion batteries.

Fuel cells are the most recent battery invention. Fuel cells work by combining hydrogen and oxygen to create electricity. One of the advantages of fuel cells is that they last much longer than other batteries. Chemicals constantly flow into the cell, keeping it charged. Fuel cells also pack more power than other batteries and are more efficient. However, hydrogen isn't a convenient fuel source at this time, so the use of fuel cells is limited. Scientists continue to work on ways to make fuel cells a more practical battery choice for the future.

CHAPTER 5

Living and Growing Chemical Energy

PLANTS IN ACTION

When a plant needs food, does it cook itself a meal or run to the nearest restaurant? No, it creates its own food. Plants are great energy convertors. They take light energy from the Sun and turn it into chemical energy. This process is called **photosynthesis**. The chemical energy from photosynthesis is used by the plant for growth and survival.

A chemical called *chlorophyll* is stored in **chloroplasts** in plants' leaves. Plants take in water from the ground and carbon dioxide from the air. In the presence of light, a chemical reaction takes place in the chloroplasts. The chemical energy stored in the leaves is changed into sugar (glucose) and oxygen. The oxygen is released into the air. The plant uses the sugar as food. Extra sugar is stored in the plant. When humans or animals eat plant products, they consume this stored chemical energy.

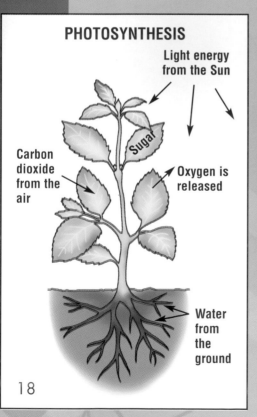

PHOTOSYNTHESIS

Light energy from the Sun

Sugar

Carbon dioxide from the air

Oxygen is released

Water from the ground

Double Duty

In addition to absorbing sunlight for photosynthesis, chlorophyll is also the material that makes plants green.

Other Food Makers

Plants are not the only living things that can make their own food. Some **bacteria** and protists (pond-water creatures) also contain chlorophyll to carry out photosynthesis. A few bacteria don't even need light to make food. They consume chemicals that are available to them as their source of energy. This is very practical at the bottom of the ocean where sunlight isn't available.

Tube worms live near hydrothermal vents on the ocean floor. Bacteria living inside the worms change chemicals in the warm water into food for the tube worms.

FOOD FOR THOUGHT

Animals, including humans, use food as fuel for their bodies. Food contains chemical energy. Since the food you eat comes from plants or animals that eat plants, the chemical energy stored in plants is in the foods you eat. This food combines with oxygen in your body and undergoes chemical reactions. The resulting chemical energy is changed to other forms of energy that your body needs. For example, heat energy keeps you warm, while motion energy allows you to move.

Calories are a measure of how much potential energy a food has. The more calories a food has, the more potential energy it provides for your body. If the food you eat has more calories than your body "burns" through activity, the extra calories are used to make fat.

Inquire and Investigate: Nutty Energy

REQUIRES ADULT SUPERVISION

Question: Does a peanut or a cashew have more chemical energy?

Answer the question: I think a _____ has more chemical energy.

Form a hypothesis: A _____ has more chemical energy.

Test the hypothesis:

Materials
- aluminum pie pan
- large paper clip
- one large peanut
- one cashew (approximately the same size as the peanut)
- clean, empty tin can
- tap water
- liquid measuring cup
- clamp
- matches or other source of fire/flame
- thermometer

Procedure
* Bend the paper clip into a stand for the nuts. Set the peanut on the stand and place it in the pie pan.

* Measure out 4 ounces of water. Pour it into the can. Record the starting temperature of the water.

* Carefully light the peanut on fire. Immediately clamp the can of water an inch above the burning nut.

* Monitor the temperature of the water until it reaches its peak (highest temperature). Record this temperature.

* When the peanut is done burning (or you've reached a peak temperature), sprinkle it with water to cool it and remove anything that's left from the stand.

* Place the cashew on the stand and repeat the burning procedure. (Make sure you empty and refill the can with new water.) Record the highest temperature of the cashew water. Compare the two temperatures.

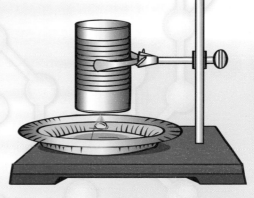

Observations: The temperature of the water from the peanut is lower than that of the water from the cashew.

Conclusions: A cashew has more chemical energy than a peanut. The greater amount of chemical energy produced more heat energy when burned, increasing the temperature of the water. This also means that cashews have more food calories than peanuts.

CHAPTER 6

Energy on the Glow

What do glow sticks, criminal investigators, and fireflies have in common? They all use chemical energy to get their work done.

A COOL KIND OF LIGHT

Chemiluminescence is the giving off of light caused by a chemical reaction. This reaction changes the chemical energy in an object to light energy. However, unlike other chemical reactions, chemiluminescence does not produce heat energy. So the light given off is a cool light.

Light sticks and glow jewelry give off light when a chemical reaction occurs inside them. Bending the plastic tubes causes a glass container inside to break. A chemical called an *activator* is then free to mix with other chemicals and a dye in the plastic tube. This chemical reaction produces a glow of light. The color of the light depends on the color of the dye.

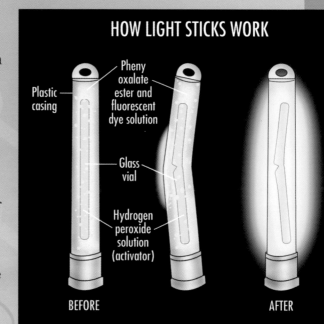

HOW LIGHT STICKS WORK

Plastic casing

Pheny oxalate ester and fluorescent dye solution

Glass vial

Hydrogen peroxide solution (activator)

BEFORE

AFTER

Inquire and Investigate: Light Sticks

Question: How does temperature affect the length and brightness of a light stick's glow?

Answer the question: I think _____.

Form a hypothesis: _____ temperatures produce a shorter, brighter glow. _____ temperatures produce a longer, dimmer glow.

Test the hypothesis:

Materials
- three light sticks of the same type, size, and color
- three clear glasses
- water (refrigerated, at room temperature, and hot)
- thermometer

Procedure
* Fill one glass with water that has been refrigerated, one with water at room temperature, and one with hot water (not boiling). Place an unactivated stick in each glass and wait ten minutes.

* Remove the light sticks from the water and activate them. Observe and compare the brightness of the glow in each one.

* Record how long each light stick glows.

Observations: The glow of each light stick decreases as the temperature of the water decreases. The colder the water, the dimmer the glow. The length of time each light stick glows decreases with each increase in water temperature. The warmer the water, the shorter the glow.

Conclusions: Warmer temperatures produce a brighter glow that lasts a shorter amount of time. Colder temperatures produce a dimmer glow that lasts longer. This is because warmer temperatures speed up the chemical reaction, so the light energy given off is more concentrated. However, the rapid reaction uses up the chemicals in the stick faster, so the length of glow time is shorter. The opposite is true with cooler temperatures. The reaction time is slower, so the light is dimmer, but the chemicals last longer, making the glow last longer as well.

You may enjoy watching crime scene investigation shows on television or reading books about how the latest scientific technology is used to catch criminals. Some of the techniques used in these investigations involve chemiluminescence. Chemiluminescence can make "invisible" blood evidence visible to the human eye. The chemicals luminol or fluorescein react with blood. When these chemical are sprayed at a crime scene, blood traces will glow faintly in a dimly lit room. The chemiluminescent chemicals react with the iron in blood to produce light energy that can incriminate a suspect.

During a murder trial, a crime scene investigator places arrows on a diagram to show where bloody footprints were revealed by luminol.

LIVING LIGHT

Many animals have chemicals in their bodies that produce light. When a chemiluminescent reaction occurs in a living thing, it's called **bioluminescence**. Most bioluminescent **organisms** make chemicals from the food they eat. These chemicals usually include luciferin and luciferase. A third chemical is often involved as well. This chemical varies depending on the creature.

Glow-in-the-Dark Bacteria

A few bioluminescent organisms get their light from glowing bacteria that live inside them. The organisms provide food for the bacteria, and the bacteria provide light to help the organisms find food, attract mates, or protect themselves. It's a perfect partnership!

Bioluminescence occurs in all colors. However, light emitted from land animals is usually yellow or green, while light emitted from sea animals is usually blue or blue-green.

Bioluminescence is helpful to a species' survival. The light helps animals find food and mates. It can also be used as a defense against enemies.

Bigfin reef squid

An amazing number of animals are bioluminescent. Fireflies are perhaps the most well-known of these creatures. In fireflies, a flash of light is created when oxygen comes in contact with chemicals in the flies' lower abdomens. Male and female fireflies use these light flashes to communicate with each other.

Bioluminescence is important in the ocean. At the water's surface, sunlight makes photosynthesis possible and vision clear. But in deeper waters, creatures are left in the dark to find their own food, mates, and safety. Glow worms, anglerfish, and flashlight fish use their bioluminescence to attract meals. Bermuda fireworms and lanternfish use light to attract mates. Some squid and shrimp shoot out clouds of light to escape from predators.

Light that filters down from the water's surface can spotlight fish and make them targets for predators. A variety of fish, shrimp, and squid produce light on their bellies that helps them blend in better. These lights replace the light from above, which is blocked by the creature's body. This reduces the animal's visibility. This form of camouflage is called *counterillumination*.

Bioluminescent cup coral polyps

Technology Link

While no plants are known to naturally produce bioluminescent light, technology has made it possible for two plants to glow in the dark. Scientists in Singapore took genes from fireflies and inserted them into orchid plants. The genes contained the code for forming luciferase. When luciferin was added to the plant, the flowers produced a light green glow. A similar experiment at the University of California in San Diego resulted in glow-in-the-dark tobacco plants. These bioluminescent successes have helped scientists isolate the genes that are responsible for bioluminescence in animals.

Firefly

A GLOWING REPORT ON CHEMICAL ENERGY

From light sticks at the county fair to crime labs in the big city, chemical energy keeps us on the glow. This energy powers our bodies, our homes, our cars, and our gadgets. Without chemical energy, there would be no burning, no photosynthesizing, and no exploding. The world would be a very dull place without this important form of energy.

Internet Connections and Related Reading for Chemical Energy

http://www.howstuffworks.com
Find out more about how chemical energy "stuff" works.
Search key words such as *batteries*, *fire*, *explosives*,
chemiluminescence, *engine*, *light sticks*, *fuel cells*, and
fireworks for more information on these topics and more.

http://www.energyquest.ca.gov/story/index.html
Get the story on energy. Read chapters 1 and 5 to learn
more about what energy is, how it's stored, how it changes
forms, and how chemical energy is used in batteries.

http://www.energizer.com/learning/default.asp
Check out Energizer's learning center to find out more about
batteries—how they work, their history, and their power.

http://www.biolum.org/
Explore bioluminescence by digging deeper into the what,
how, and why of this living light.

**http://www.bbc.co.uk/science/genes/gene_safari/wild_west/
glowing_gallery.shtml**
Glow-in-the-dark mice, green glowing bunnies—you won't
believe your eyes! See some of the advancements being
made in the area of bioluminescence for yourself.

Energy by Jack Challoner. An Eyewitness Science book on energy. Millbrook Press, 1993. [RL 7.9 IL 3–8] (5868601 PB 5868606 HB)

The Nature and Science of Fire by Jane Burton and Kim Taylor. This book explores fire—how it burns and what impact it has on nature. Gareth Stevens, 2001. [RL 6.1 IL 2–6] (6875806 HB)

Photosynthesis by Alvin and Virginia Silverstein and Laura Silverstein Nunn. Explains the fundamental concept of photosynthesis, gives some background, and discusses current applications and developments. Millbrook Press, 1998. [RL 5 IL 5–8] (3112206 HB)

•RL = Reading Level
•IL = Interest Level
Perfection Learning's catalog numbers are included for your ordering convenience. PB indicates paperback. HB indicates hardback.

Glossary

atom (AT uhm) tiny particle that makes up everything in the world

bacteria (bak TEER ee uh) common single-celled organism

battery (BAT er ee) device that stores chemical energy and changes it into electrical energy

bioluminescence (beye oh loom uh NES ens) the giving off of light by a living thing

chemical (KEM uh kuhl) one of the basic substances that make up all things

chemical bond (KEM uh kuhl bahnd) force that holds the atoms and molecules in a chemical together (see separate entries for *atom* and *molecule*)

chemical energy (KEM uh kuhl EN er jee) energy stored within chemical bonds and released during chemical reactions (see separate entries for *chemical bond* and *chemical reaction*)

chemical reaction (KEM uh kuhl ree AK shuhn) the breaking and forming of chemical bonds to create new substances (see separate entry for *chemical bond*)

chemiluminescence (kem ee loo muh NES ens) the giving off of light caused by a chemical reaction (see separate entry for *chemical reaction*)

chloroplast (KLOR uh plast) cell in a plant that stores chlorophyll and is the site of photosynthesis (see separate entry for *photosynthesis*)

combustion (kuhm BUS chuhn) burning; chemical reaction between a fuel and oxygen that produces light and heat energy (see separate entry for *chemical reaction*)

element (EL uh ment) nonliving material made up of one type of atom (see separate entry for *atom*)

energy (EN er jee) ability to do work

explosion (ek SPLOH zhuhn) sudden release of a large amount of energy

flammable (FLAM uh buhl) able to burn easily

Industrial Revolution (in DUH stree uhl rev uh LOO shuhn) period during the late 1800s where industry increased greatly in Europe and the United States

molecule (MAHL uh kyoul) tiny particle of a substance made up of two or more atoms (see separate entry for *atom*)

organism (OR guh niz uhm) living thing

photosynthesis (foh toh SIN thuh sis) chemical process by which plants and other organisms produce food using chemical and solar energy

vapor (VAY per) gaseous form of a liquid or solid

Index